GERMANY

...in Pictures

Prepared by
Geography Department

Lerner Publications Company
Minneapolis

Courtesy of German Information Center

**Pickers harvest wine grapes along the steep banks of the
Rhine River in western Germany.**

This book is an all-new edition in the Visual Geography Series. Previous editions were published by
Sterling Publishing Company, New York City. The
text, set in 10/12 Century Textbook, is fully revised
and updated, and new photographs, maps, charts,
and captions have been added.

Website address: www.lernerbooks.com

LIBRARY OF CONGRESS CATALOGING-IN-PUBLICATION DATA

Germany in pictures / prepared by Geography Depart-
    ment, Lerner Publications Company, Minneapolis.
    p.   cm—(Visual geography series)
    Includes index.
    ISBN 0–8225–1873–2 (lib. bdg.)
    1. Germany. [1. Germany] I. Lerner Publications
Company. Geography Dept. II. Series: Visual geography series (Minneapolis, Minn.)
DD17.G48   1994
943—dc20   93–40971

International Standard Book Number: 0–8225–1873–2
Library of Congress Catalog Card Number: 93–40971

VISUAL GEOGRAPHY SERIES®

Publisher
Harry Jonas Lerner
Senior Editor
Mary M. Rodgers
Editors
Tom Streissguth
Colleen Sexton
Photo Researcher
Erica Ackerberg
Editorial/Photo Assistant
Marybeth Campbell
Consultants/Contributors
Carlienne Fresch
Gerhard Weiss
Sebastian Gutmann
Sandra K. Davis
Designer
Jim Simondet
Cartographer
Carol F. Barrett
Indexer
Sylvia Timian
Production Manager
Gary J. Hansen

Independent Picture Service

**Rowers glide along a canal in the German *land* (state) of
Brandenburg.**

Acknowledgments

Title page photo © Steven C. Hankins.

Elevation contours adapted from *The Times Atlas of
the World,* seventh comprehensive edition (New York:
Times Books, 1985).

2   3   4   5   6   7   –   JR   –   03   02   01   00   99   98

Young Germans gather newspapers and bottles for recycling. Germany's government has adopted a nationwide plan for the collection of many household items that can be recycled or reused.

Contents

NORTH SEA

BALTIC SEA

NORTH FRISIAN IS.

DENMARK

EAST FRISIAN IS.

NETHERLANDS

Wilhelmshaven

Kiel Canal

Kiel

Rostock

Hamburg

Lake Schaal

Lake Müritz

Bremerhaven

Bremen

Weser R.

Elbe R.

Havel R.

Oder R.

Canal

Hanover

Canal

Mittelland

BERLIN

Potsdam

Spree R.

BRANDENBURG

POLAND

WESTPHALIA

Ruhr R.

RUHR

Düsseldorf

Cologne

Aachen

Bonn

Rhine R.

BELGIUM

LUXEMBOURG

Cochem

Mosel R.

Trier

SAAR

Frankfurt

Mannheim

Heidelberg

FRANCONIA

FRANCE

ALSACE-LORRAINE

Rothenburg

THURINGIA

Weimar

Leipzig

SAXONY

Meissen

Dresden

SILESIA

CZECH REPUBLIC

Bamberg

Bayreuth

Main R.

Regnitz R.

Dinkelsbühl

Stuttgart

Neckar R.

Danube R.

Canal

SWABIA

BAVARIA

Munich

Bodensee

Oberammergau

Garmisch-Partenkirchen

SWITZERLAND

AUSTRIA

GERMANY

N

State Boundaries

Major Roads

0	50	100 Miles
0	50	100 Kilometers

EUROPE
GERMANY

0   400 Miles
0   400 Kilometers

Arctic Circle

20°   0°   20°

NORWEGIAN SEA

NORTH ATLANTIC OCEAN

60°

60°

20°

40°

40°

MEDITERRANEAN SEA

0°

20°

METRIC CONVERSION CHART
To Find Approximate Equivalents

WHEN YOU KNOW:	MULTIPLY BY:	TO FIND:
acres	0.41	hectares
square miles	2.59	square kilometers
CAPACITY		
gallons	3.79	liters
LENGTH		
feet	30.48	centimeters
yards	0.91	meters
miles	1.61	kilometers
MASS (weight)		
pounds	0.45	kilograms
tons	0.91	metric tons
VOLUME		
cubic yards	0.77	cubic meters
TEMPERATURE		
degrees Fahrenheit	0.56 (*after* subtracting 32)	degrees Celsius

Old houses line the Weinmarkt, a street in the center of Dinkelsbühl. The winding streets and traditional architecture of this town have made it a favorite destination for foreign tourists.

Photo © Don Eastman

Introduction

Located in north central Europe, Germany is one of the continent's largest and most populous nations. Although the country has suffered division and destruction, its people claim a long history and a rich cultural heritage. Germany has produced many renowned writers, scientists, musicians, and philosophers. In recent times, Germany's productive industries have also made it one of the world's leading economic powers.

Nomadic peoples of northern Europe first settled Germany's dense forests and river valleys. In the late eighth century A.D., the emperor Charlemagne united these groups under his rule. After Charlemagne's death, local barons and dukes established semi-independent principalities (realms of princes) in the eastern part of the empire.

These realms later became a part of the Holy Roman Empire, a confederation of

The glass walls of the Eurohaus in Frankfurt reflect the extensive reconstruction of Germany after World War II (1939–1945). The country's architects used modern materials and designs to rebuild areas that were destroyed during the war.

states in central Europe and northern Italy. For centuries all the Holy Roman emperors came from the Habsburg family—a wealthy, ethnically German dynasty (family of rulers). Yet Germany itself remained a patchwork of semi-independent cities and states with their own rulers, laws, and customs. In the early nineteenth century, as the armies of the French emperor Napoleon Bonaparte entered Germany, the Holy Roman Empire collapsed.

Otto von Bismarck, a strong-willed politician from Prussia (northern Germany), united the German states into a new empire in the late 1800s. The German Empire developed its industries and built factories, ships, and a modern transportation system. Germany also used much of its growing wealth to strengthen its armed forces.

A teacher instructs an attentive pupil at a state-owned vocational center, where students train for careers in manufacturing.

More than 500,000 runners participated in the 1988 Berlin Peace Run.

According to a tradition of the Harz region of Germany, newly married couples saw a piece of wood after their wedding ceremony.

Seeking to increase its power in Europe, Germany fought two world wars in the twentieth century. Allied armies defeated Germany in both conflicts. After World War II (1939-1945), the Allies occupied Germany and divided the nation—and its capital, Berlin—into western and eastern zones. West Germany established a democratic government. In East Germany, a Communist regime seized most private property and began a system of central economic planning.

In 1990 Germany reunited after the collapse of Communist rule in eastern Europe. The West German government extended its constitution, currency, and laws to eastern Germany. Since then supply and demand determine wages, prices, and production throughout Germany.

In the late 1990s, Germany was still reeling after uniting its two economies. Many companies had collapsed, and unemployment was at record levels. Shifting politics had stalled government efforts at economic reform. Meanwhile, many Germans have noticed a violent, anti-foreign undercurrent in their society, directed especially at immigrants from southern Europe and the Middle East. Although Germany is one of Europe's most prosperous nations, it faces difficult social problems and an uncertain future.

The Bavarian Alps tower over the fields and valleys of Garmisch-Partenkirchen. This region near Germany's border with Switzerland hosted the 1936 Winter Olympics.

1) The Land

Germany's landscape includes flat plains, rolling hills, wide river valleys, sandy coasts, and rugged mountain ranges. Once covered by an immense forest, the nation has cut down most of its woodlands to provide land for cities, industrial zones, and farms. With a total land area of 137,854 square miles, Germany is slightly smaller than the state of Montana.

Germany shares borders with Denmark in the north and with Austria and Switzerland in the south. To the west of Germany are the Netherlands, Belgium, Luxembourg, and France. On the east lie Poland and the Czech Republic. Germany has coasts that touch the Baltic Sea in the northeast and the North Sea in the northwest.

Topography

The major land regions of Germany run in roughly parallel, east-west bands across the country. Ancient glaciers (ice masses) once covered the largest and northernmost region, the North German Plain. As the glaciers melted, they left behind flat lowlands, small lakes, and heaths (areas of sandy, infertile soil). Broad rivers flow northward through the plain, and swamps

8

A farmer marches through his vineyard along a narrow path.

and bogs have formed in areas of poor drainage. Off the northwestern coast of Germany are the flat, sandy East Frisian Islands and North Frisian Islands.

Although much of the soil in the North German Plain is too poor for crop production, livestock graze on pastures in the region, and local tree farms supply Germany's lumber mills. The southern edge of the plain contains fertile areas known as *borden,* where farmers can raise a variety of grain and vegetable crops.

More than a dozen small mountain ranges rise within the Central Highlands, a region stretching across the middle of Germany. Brocken, a mountain peak, reaches 3,747 feet within the Harz range, which straddles the old boundary between

The old center of Heidelberg rises on the banks of the Neckar River in central Germany. The Germans built many of their cities along waterways, which once provided the fastest and safest route for transporting people and goods through central Europe.

9

Cross-country skiers stop to rest in the forests of south-eastern Germany. Sturdy wooden signs guide the millions of hikers and skiers who use Germany's public recreation areas each year.

East and West Germany. Dense woodlands, including the Thuringian and Bohemian forests, cover the mountains and the broad valleys to the south. The fertile Thuringian Basin, in eastern Germany, ends at the Ore Mountains on the border of the Czech Republic.

Long, wooded ridges are common in the South German Hills. The steep Swabian Jura (highland) runs north of the Danube River near the river's source in southwestern Germany. The Franconian Jura, the

Houses line the Regnitz River in Bamberg, a city in Bavaria. The historic center of Bamberg lies on an island in the river.

The Elbe River flows past steep cliffs and cultivated fields near Dresden in eastern Germany. After a 724-mile journey, the river empties into the North Sea.

Steigerwald, and other highlands rise above plateaus and winding river valleys. The clay soil of the region provides fertile farmland. The mountainous Black Forest, in southwestern Germany, takes its name from the thick forests of fir and spruce trees that cover the hillsides.

The Alpine Forelands (foothills) begin south of the Danube and continue to the Bavarian Alps, which rise along Germany's borders with Switzerland and Austria. Ancient glaciers formed many lakes in southern Bavaria, an area of rapid streams, rolling foothills, pastures, and fields of wheat and other grains. Southwest of Munich—the largest city in southern Germany—rises Zugspitze (9,721 feet), the country's highest point.

Rivers and Lakes

For centuries Germany's waterways provided an important transportation link for its many principalities and trading centers. German cities used the rivers to ship their products to market, and the more powerful states collected river tolls. In modern times, a system of canals has brought many of Germany's major rivers into a Europeanwide shipping network.

The Rhine River rises in the Swiss Alps, flows northward, and for many miles forms a natural border between Germany and its neighbors Switzerland and France. After passing the industrial Ruhr region of western Germany, the river enters the Netherlands and empties into the North Sea.

One of the busiest water routes in the world, the Rhine accommodates 9,000 cargo vessels each month. Commercial boats can navigate about 500 miles of the Rhine's 820-mile length. Cruise ships and sightseeing boats carry vacationers up and down the river to view the castles, villages, and vineyards of the Rhine valley.

A canal now links the Rhine to the Main and Danube rivers, allowing ships to travel from the North Sea, an arm of the Atlantic Ocean, to the Black Sea in southeastern Europe. The Danube—the only major river in Germany to flow eastward—passes through southern Germany before crossing into Austria. Engineers have built canals and deep channels that enable barges to navigate the river's course.

The rivers of the North German Plain empty into either the North Sea or the Baltic Sea, which are linked by the Kiel Canal. The Weser River passes the busy port of Bremen, and the Elbe flows through Hamburg before widening into a broad estuary. Canals join the Rhine with these two waterways and with the Oder River, part of which divides Germany from Poland.

The glaciers that once covered Germany carved many basins in which small lakes formed. Lake Müritz, Lake Schwerin, and several other glacial lakes dot the North German Plain. Germany, Switzerland, and Austria line the shores of Lake Constance

Colorful flowering trees brighten a hillside in southern Germany. Although the building of cities, freeways, and factories has destroyed much of Germany's natural landscape, strict laws protect the remaining forests from logging and development.

(also known as the Bodensee), which is about 45 miles long and 10 miles wide. The level of the lake rises in the spring, when ice and snow melt in the nearby Alps.

Climate

Extreme temperatures are rare in Germany, which has a mild continental climate. Easterly winds bring warm summers and cold winters to the plains of eastern Germany. Temperatures in the capital of Berlin, a northeastern city, average 69° F in July, the warmest month, and 30° F in January, the coldest month. The weather is milder in western Germany, where winds blowing from the Atlantic Ocean heat the air in the winter and cool it in summer.

Highland regions, including the Harz Mountains and the Bavarian Alps, often experience below-freezing winter temperatures. The high altitude of the Alps shortens the mountain summers, but an Alpine wind called the *föhn* can bring warm, clear weather to southern Germany in any season. Temperatures in Munich average 63° F in July and 28° F in January.

Rain falls throughout the year in the northwest, but farther inland most rain occurs in summer. The mountains of the south may receive more than 80 inches of rain and snow a year, while about 30 inches of precipitation falls annually in the Central Highlands. During winter, ice clogs Germany's seaports, and snow blankets the peaks and valleys of the Bavarian Alps.

Flora and Fauna

Centuries of settlement and farming have greatly reduced Germany's woodlands. Natural forests and cultivated plantations now cover about one-third of the land. Pine trees grow in the sandy soil of the coastal region, while stands of spruce dominate the woods of the Central Highlands. Silver firs flourish in the mountains of the south and in the Black Forest.

Strict laws require that all trees harvested for timber in Germany must be replaced. Nevertheless, the nation's forests diminished during the 1980s, when air pollution caused many trees to lose their foliage and die.

There is little ground vegetation in Germany's tree plantations, but the country's

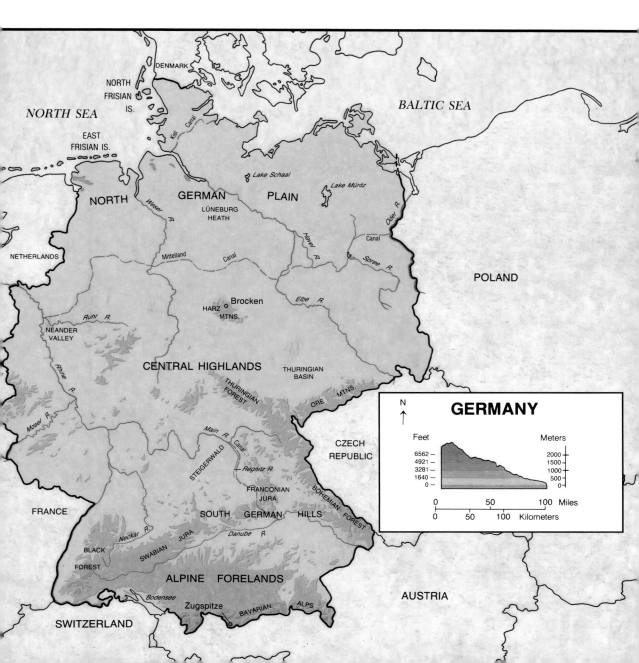

natural forests contain heather, mosses, and lichens. Broom, juniper, and bracken plants grow in the heaths of the north. During late spring, wildflowers color the slopes of the Bavarian Alps.

Germany is home to many native species of animals and birds. Deer, lynx, pine martens, and grouse survive in the country's forests. Beavers live in the Elbe valley, and wild boars and deer roam the woodlands of Bavaria. The Lüneburg Heath and many of the surrounding heaths in the North German Plain are protected game reserves. A 5,680-acre area along Lake Schaal in eastern Germany is inhabited by sea eagles, cranes, cormorants, ospreys, and other birds.

Natural Resources

Germany has a variety of natural resources, but coal is the only mineral found in large quantities. The Ruhr contains major deposits of coal, although mining operations have exhausted many of the largest pits in the region. Coal also exists in the Saar region west of the Rhine River. Workers mine lignite (brown) coal near Cologne in the Rhine valley, in Bavaria, and in eastern Germany.

The Harz Mountains and the Thuringian Forest contain significant deposits of iron ore, an important ingredient of steel production. Deposits of potash east of the Harz region make Germany one of the world's largest suppliers of this valuable fertilizer. Engineers have discovered oil reserves near the North Sea coast, but Germany still must import most of its oil and natural gas.

Germany's other natural resources include rock salt, copper, lead, silver, tin, uranium, zinc, and bauxite (the raw material of aluminum). Artisans use ka-

At an open-pit coal mine in eastern Germany, engineers watch the progress of a gigantic crane.

A boy hammers out a souvenir from the remains of the Berlin Wall. The fall of this concrete barrier in 1989 allowed Berliners to travel freely again throughout their city.

Photo © Ed King

The Communist government built a massive wall around West Berlin in 1961 to prevent East Germans from fleeing to West Germany. In 1989, when the East German government opened its borders, the Berlin Wall was destroyed. Soon the two Germanies reunited, and the nation began planning to transfer the federal government back to Berlin from Bonn, in western Germany.

Although World War II bombing heavily damaged the city, a few landmarks survived. The State Opera House and the State Library date to the 1700s. The imposing Reichstag was built in the late nineteenth century as the seat of Germany's parliament. Near the Kurfürstendamm, the main street of western Berlin, stand

olin, a fine white clay, to make the country's famous Dresden china.

Berlin

Located on Germany's northeastern plains, Berlin (population 3.4 million) began in the 1200s as the two towns of Berlin and Kölln. Lying on opposite banks of the Spree River, these busy trade centers merged in 1397. In 1701 Berlin became the administrative hub of the German kingdom of Prussia. After the founding of the German Empire in 1871, the city served as the national capital until 1945.

After Germany's defeat in World War II, four foreign powers—the United States, Britain, France, and the Soviet Union—occupied Berlin. The city was later divided into eastern and western sectors. East Berlin became the capital of Communist East Germany. West Berlin remained part of West Germany, although it was cut off from the rest of that country.

Independent Picture Service

The towers of the twelfth-century Church of St. Nicholas dominate the Nikolai quarter of eastern Berlin. The church, which was destroyed during World War II, was rebuilt according to original architectural plans after the war.

Photo by Erwin C. "Bud" Nielsen

Diners crowd a busy sidewalk cafe in Munich. The largest city in southern Germany, Munich is famous for art, music, theater, and beer.

the walls of the Kaiser Wilhelm Church. Partially destroyed by bombing, the church's ruins were left in place as a powerful reminder of the war.

A major manufacturing center, Berlin produces electronics, machinery, chemicals, steel, clothing, textiles, and rubber goods. A canal links a busy industrial port on the Spree River to the North and Baltic seas. The capital also has important civilian and military airports and is a major railroad hub for northern Europe.

Secondary Cities

Germany's cities began growing rapidly in the 1800s, as new industries attracted job-seekers from the countryside. Although many urban centers were heavily damaged during World War II, the postwar recovery, especially in West Germany, allowed the large cities to rebuild. City dwellers make up 85 percent of the total German population—one of the highest urban concentrations in Europe.

Hamburg (population 1.6 million) lies on the Elbe River in northwestern Germany. The city was founded as Hammaburg in A.D. 810 by the emperor Charlemagne. In the twelfth century, Hamburg joined the Hanseatic League, a trade association of northern European cities. Although the

Photo © Luke Golobitsh

A stone bear welcomes visitors at the gates of the Berlin Zoo.

league later disbanded, Germany's principal seaport has kept its historic name as the Free and Hanseatic City of Hamburg.

Shipyards, ironworks, steelworks, sawmills, and manufacturing facilities operate in Hamburg's industrial areas. Other plants make chemicals and optical instruments. Although the city has large factory districts and extensive port facilities, nearly half of its land is covered by greenery and parks.

The capital of Bavaria, Munich (population 1.3 million) is known as München to German-speakers. The city enjoys a lively cultural life and supports concert halls, jazz clubs, art galleries, and theaters. It is also the center of Germany's huge beer industry. Oktoberfest, Munich's annual beer festival, attracts visitors from around the world. The city also produces automobiles, aircraft, and electronic equipment.

Cologne (population 963,000), one of Germany's oldest cities, was first settled by the Ubii, an ancient Germanic group. The most famous landmark of Cologne is

Photo by Erwin C. "Bud" Nielsen

Passenger ferries and barges dock along the banks of the Rhine River in Cologne.

a towering cathedral that took more than 600 years to build. The city's factories make chemicals, textiles, automobiles, and

Independent Picture Service

Many German cities prohibit motorized vehicles from pedestrian malls, where shoppers and strollers mingle on wide, clean sidewalks.

In 1951, six years after World War II ended, much of central Dresden still lay in ruins from a devastating bombing raid.

chocolate. Eau de Cologne, a well-known fragrance, was invented in Cologne in the eighteenth century.

Many Habsburg emperors were crowned in the cathedral of Frankfurt (population 656,000), but this city on the Main River also served as the seat of Germany's first elected parliament. An important commercial and industrial hub, Frankfurt has factories that make leather goods, chemicals, and pharmaceuticals. Germany's central bank and stock exchange have their headquarters in Frankfurt, which has become the nation's financial capital. An international book fair in the city attracts thousands of editors, writers, and publishers each year.

Settled in the tenth century, Dresden (population 478,000) later served as the capital of Saxony, a powerful German state. A city of fine churches and imposing palaces, Dresden also became a manufacturing center in the late 1800s. But the city was devastated in February 1945, when air raids reduced most of Dresden's buildings to rubble. Architects are painstakingly rebuilding many churches and monuments. Since 1713, factories in the nearby town of Meissen have produced the world famous Dresden china, the first porcelain made in Europe.

About 60 miles northwest of Dresden is Leipzig (population 489,000), which occupies a strategic junction of rivers and railroads. An early center of the German publishing industry, Leipzig also hosts a trade fair that attracts manufacturers from throughout the world. Factories in the city produce steel, chemicals, plastics, textiles, and clothing.

Modern shops and office buildings eventually replaced many of Dresden's destroyed buildings. At left stands the Panorama, a popular movie theater.

An ancient Celt handcrafted this pitcher in the form of a bird. Skilled farmers and metalsmiths, the Celts were the first group to establish towns in the dense forests of north central Europe.

2) History and Government

Archaeologists believe that human beings have lived in Germany for about 650,000 years, but very little is known about the region's first inhabitants. As early as 100,000 years ago, nomadic hunting groups migrated into the forests and river valleys of north central europe. The remains of one of these early hunters have been found in the Neander Valley near Düsseldorf. The discovery led scientists to name these prehistoric people Neanderthals.

By 400 B.C., groups of Celts had settled much of central Europe, including southern and western Germany. They raised grains and livestock and crafted iron tools and weapons for use in farming and in warfare. The Celts also mastered the refining of metal ores into gold, silver, and bronze.

Teutonic Settlers

Around 100 B.C., northern European peoples known as Teutons migrated southward into Germany, pushing aside the Celts. At the same time, the armies of Rome, an expanding empire based on the Italian Peninsula, were conquering Celtic groups west of the Rhine River. This

19

Photo by Drs. A. A. M. van der Heyden, Naarden, the Netherlands

The Romans built the Black Gate to defend Trier, Germany's oldest city. The gate's two open ports lured attackers into a courtyard, where soldiers could strike from the overhanging walls.

mighty waterway later divided the Roman province of Gaul (modern France) and Germania, the Roman name for Teutonic lands lying east of the Rhine.

The dense forests of Germania slowed the Roman attacks on Teutonic farms and villages. Unable to conquer the region, the Romans built a line of fortifications between the Rhine and the Danube to prevent Teutonic invasions of Gaul and Italy.

By the fourth century A.D., however, raids from Germania were weakening Rome. In A.D. 395, the empire was divided into eastern and western halves. Many of the Germanic groups—including the Goths and the Franks—saw this as an opportunity to press their attacks. In 410 the Goths invaded Italy, burning and pillaging the city of Rome, the capital of the western empire.

To strengthen his forces, the Roman emperor hired Germanic soldiers to serve in the Roman army under Germanic commanders. But Odoacer, one of these leaders, turned against Rome in 476. As his troops attacked the capital, Odoacer deposed the emperor and became the ruler of Italy. The western empire collapsed, and the Franks and other Germanic groups began crossing the Rhine and seizing Roman territory in Gaul.

Early Kingdoms

In 486 the Frankish king Clovis defeated the Roman governor who was still ruling in Gaul. After his victory, Clovis established the Frankish Empire, a realm that stretched across much of northern Europe. He also converted his subjects to Chris-

A statue of the Frankish emperor Charlemagne stands in the Römerberg, a central square of Frankfurt.

Photo by Erwin C. "Bud" Nielsen

tianity, a faith introduced to Europe from the Middle East. In religious matters, the Franks submitted to the Roman Catholic pope, the head of the Christian church in Rome.

After the death of Clovis, the empire was divided among his sons, an act that weakened the realm. Many of the Germanic groups began to claim independence from Frankish rule. In northern Germany, for example, the powerful Saxons remained independent and strongly opposed to Christianity.

Charlemagne, who became the ruler of the Franks in 768, defeated the Saxons and greatly expanded his realm in central and western Europe. In 800 Pope Leo III crowned Charlemagne as "Emperor of the

Towers and gates surround the town of Rothenburg. With no central government or national army to protect them, ancient German cities had to build their own strong defenses against attack.

Courtesy of Minneapolis Public Library and Information Center

Romans," and the Frankish king became the ruler of a revived western empire. For a few years, Charlemagne united the Germanic peoples and ended the frequent warfare and invasions in western Europe.

Charlemagne established a central administration from his capital at Aachen. A progressive leader, he also ordered the building of schools and monasteries to encourage education and scholarship. Under Charlemagne's supervision, scholars prepared the first dictionary of the German language.

After Charlemagne's death, his heirs fought among themselves for control of the realm. In 843 three of Charlemagne's grandsons signed the Treaty of Verdun, which divided the empire. Ludwig II took East Francia, which included territory east of the Rhine River. Lothair gained the Middle Kingdom, a smaller realm lying west of the Rhine. Charles I (the Bold) ruled West Francia, which later became the kingdom of France.

During the ninth century, raiders from the east staged several attacks on East Francia. For their help in defending the realm, German nobles received titles and land from their king. Gradually, these nobles, or dukes, created independent

Photo by Bildarchiv Preussischer Kulturbesitz

Saint Boniface, known as the "apostle of the Germans," converted the Saxons of northern Germany to the Christian faith in the eighth century.

Old German homes were built with frames of thick, heavy beams. The wood and mortar used were strong enough to last for centuries.

duchies within Germany. The largest and most powerful duchies were Saxony, Swabia, Franconia, Bavaria, and Lorraine.

The Holy Roman Empire

In 919, after the dynasty begun by Charlemagne had died out, the Frankish and Saxon nobles elected the Saxon duke Henry I as the king of Germany. Henry brought the five largest German duchies into a strong alliance. His son, Otto I, claimed extensive new lands to the west and south for the kingdom.

A brilliant military strategist, Otto stopped an invasion of his realm by the nomadic Magyars in 955. Heeding a call

After leading his forces into Italy to protect the pope, King Otto I of Germany was crowned ruler of the Holy Roman Empire, a confederacy of German and Italian states.

Ships and laborers crowd the docks of a busy port in northern Germany. The Hanseatic League united several German cities in a common trading bloc and linked German merchants to foreign markets on the North and Baltic seas.

for help by the pope, whose lands were also threatened by invasion, Otto led his forces into Italy in 962. In gratitude the pope crowned Otto as the first Holy Roman emperor. For centuries after this event, the kings of Germany also became the leaders of the Holy Roman Empire.

Under Otto's successors, the Holy Roman Empire included hundreds of large and small territories, each ruled by a member of the German nobility. The nobles—who had their own courts, laws, and armed forces—also had the power to elect the king. With no central administration or seat of power, the German kings wandered from city to city, relying on rents from their lands to support their courts.

In the mid-1100s, however, Germany was united briefly under Frederick I. Nick-named Barbarossa (meaning "red-beard"), Frederick was a strong, daring leader who became king in 1152 and Holy Roman

emperor three years later. Through military force and negotiation, Frederick extended his rule to parts of what are now Poland and Hungary. Frederick's ambitious son Henry VI also brought northern Italy into the realm.

The Hanseatic League

Under Frederick I and his son, trade and industry increased along Germany's seacoast and in lands adjoining the Rhine River. Rural laborers moved to the towns. where they became merchants, traders, and artisans. As these trading centers grew and prospered, they became wealthy enough to break free of the German princes and to become independent cities.

Representatives of several free German cities formed the Hanseatic League, or Hansa, in 1241. Founded in the German port of Lübeck, the league also included

For nine centuries, this jeweled crown was worn by the rulers of the Holy Roman Empire, many of whom were members of the powerful Habsburg dynasty (family of rulers).

Bremen, Hamburg, and Cologne. The Hansa cities developed a system of maritime and commercial laws, established banks, and set up legislatures, courts, and treasuries. The network of Hanseatic trading posts reached from England in the west to Russia and Scandinavia in the east.

While the Hansa cities flourished, the German states ruled by nobles and princes remained mostly rural and agricultural. With little trade to enrich their treasuries, these principalities battled among themselves to impose taxes, to hire soldiers, and to collect tolls on the rivers and roads.

In 1273 the German princes elected Rudolf I, a member of the powerful Habsburg family, as their king. Rudolf added to Habsburg lands by seizing Austria, a duchy lying southeast of Germany along the Danube River. Through conquests and marriage alliances, the Habsburgs greatly enlarged the territory under their control.

In the fourteenth century, Charles IV, the Habsburg king and Holy Roman emperor, issued a law called the Golden Bull. This law codified an old tradition in

A Rathaus, or town hall, dominates the central square of Rothenburg. The town's masons and carpenters finished the left half of the building in 1240. The right half, which the city rebuilt after a fire, dates to 1572.

A drawing shows the German inventor Johannes Gutenberg examining sheets turned out by his printing press. Gutenberg's new press, which was the first to use movable type, allowed religious thinkers to publish thousands of copies of their works. As a result, the writers were able to quickly spread their ideas throughout Germany.

which seven German "electors" had the power to choose the Holy Roman emperor. The law increased the power of the electors, whose lands could not be divided. The electors soon became the wealthiest rulers in the empire.

In 1438 the electors chose Albert II, a member of the Habsburg dynasty, as emperor. For the next five centuries, the imperial title would remain with the Habsburgs, who controlled Austria and other principalities that made up the realm's largest and strongest domain.

The Protestant Reformation

Important changes occurred in Germany in the fifteenth century, when a revival of ancient arts and philosophy called the Renaissance arrived from Italy. Renaissance scholars in the new German universities pressed for changes in the powerful Roman Catholic Church. One of these reformers, a German priest named Martin Luther, attacked the practices of the

Martin Luther claimed that the Roman Catholic Church, through its corrupt practices, had lost its moral authority. Luther's revolutionary ideas led to the establishment of the Lutheran Church.

church, which banned him in 1521. Many people in northern Germany, however, were joining Luther's call for reform. His followers, who were known as Protestants, established the Lutheran Church in the 1520s. Soon the Protestant Reformation was sweeping across northern Europe.

By 1555 a majority of Germans—including townspeople, nobles, and peasants—had become Protestants. Several northern German princes used the Reformation as an excuse to seize lands owned by the Catholic church. Facing a dangerous rebellion, the Catholic Habsburg emperor Charles V signed the Peace of Augsburg. This pact gave the princes the right to choose the religion of their own realms.

During the next few decades, new Protestant sects were established in Germany, the Netherlands, and Switzerland. These Reformed churches rejected both Lutheran and Catholic practices. In addition, the Roman Catholic Church won back much of southern Germany, as well as Austria and Bohemia (a kingdom lying north of Austria). The church had a strong ally in the Habsburg dynasty, whose members were loyal Catholics. But in 1618 an attempt by the Habsburgs to place a Catholic on the throne of Bohemia led to a violent uprising. This touched off a 30-year conflict between Europe's Protestants and Catholics.

During the Thirty Years' War, German princes attacked their rivals, and foreign armies marched across central Europe to seize and plunder German lands. Allying with the Protestants, the king of Sweden led an invasion of Germany's Baltic coast. French leaders sent troops across the Rhine to fight against their rivals, the Habsburgs.

In May 1618, to protest Catholic rule of Bohemia (a nation of central Europe), Protestants hurled two Catholic ministers from the windows of the royal palace of Prague, the Bohemian capital. Although the ministers survived, the incident sparked a Protestant uprising in Bohemia that led to the Thirty Years' War.

The war ended in 1648, when Protestant and Catholic leaders agreed to the Peace of Westphalia. The truce officially recognized Catholic and Protestant territories in Germany. Habsburg authority over the Protestant states ended, although members of the Habsburg dynasty still held the title of Holy Roman emperor.

The Rise of Prussia

The Peace of Westphalia strengthened the rulers of Saxony, Bavaria, Brandenburg, Prussia, and other large German states. Many of these princes began to play an important role in European conflicts over trade and territory. Meanwhile, the power of the Habsburg rulers—whose domain came to be known as Austria—began to decline.

By the early eighteenth century, the Hohenzollern dynasty ruled the combined territories of Prussia and Brandenburg in northern Germany. The Hohenzollern kings organized an efficient administration and commanded a large, professional army. In 1740 Frederick II (the Great), the king of Prussia, invaded and occupied Silesia, a mineral-rich region ruled by the Habsburgs.

Rivalry over Silesia sparked another conflict between Austria and Prussia in 1756. Frederick led his armies against Austria and its many allies, which included Russia, France, Bavaria, and Saxony. The high cost of this Seven Years' War forced Maria Theresa, the Habsburg empress, to ask for peace terms in 1763. By the Treaty of Hubertusburg, Prussia kept Silesia. Later the Hohenzollerns

Photo © Don Eastman

The Nauener Tor (gate) rises in Potsdam, a city near Berlin. The gate was designed in the mid-eighteenth century, when the Prussian king Frederick the Great was transforming Potsdam into a magnificent summer residence.

Photo by Bildarchiv Preussischer Kulturbesitz

In the 1790s, after a popular uprising toppled the monarchy of France, Germany's cities and principalities also began to suffer revolutionary violence. This engraving shows a rowdy mob demonstrating for the establishment of a German republic.

expanded their realm across northern Germany, creating the largest and most powerful German state.

Napoleonic Wars

In the early 1790s, a popular revolution brought down the king of France. Europe's rulers, who feared rebellion in their own lands, were soon at war with the French revolutionary armies. The French crossed the Rhine to occupy German principalities and to spread antimonarchy sentiment among the German people.

The French general Napoleon Bonaparte took command of his nation in 1799. Napoleon invaded Germany and defeated Prussian and Austrian armies sent against him. In 1806 Napoleon organized his German conquests into the Confederation of the Rhine, an action that destroyed the Holy Roman Empire.

The armies of Prussia, Austria, and Russia defeated the French in 1813 at Leipzig. Prussia and Britain routed Napoleon two years later at the Battle of Waterloo and forced the French leader into exile.

The victorious nations then met at the Congress of Vienna to redraw the boundaries of Europe. Prussia gained more land in northern Europe, while the Habsburgs lost territory in southern Germany. The congress also reorganized the German kingdoms, duchies, and principalities into the 39 states of the new German Confederation.

The German Confederation

Although the confederation established a national parliament, the Bundestag, this

29

legislature had little authority. Each state within the German Confederation enforced its own laws, coined its own money, collected its own taxes, and raised its own armies. In 1834 a customs union was established among most of the German states. Led by Prussia, this open market stimulated German industry and served as a model for a unified German state.

Poor harvests during the 1840s, however, led to food shortages and economic problems. Many Germans demanded the formation of a truly democratic government. In 1848 an uprising in France sparked riots in Austria and Germany. The rulers of Prussia, Bavaria, and other German states then agreed to establish a new assembly in Frankfurt.

Independent Picture Service

Military victories over Denmark, Austria, and France allowed Otto von Bismarck to forcefully unite the states of the German Confederation into a new German Empire.

The members of this legislature proposed a constitution in which Germany would be united under a hereditary emperor. The assembly offered the title of emperor to Frederick William, the king of Prussia. But Frederick William—who strongly opposed the assembly—refused the title. The assembly gradually lost support and was dissolved in 1849.

Unification

In 1862 Frederick William's successor, King Wilhelm I, appointed Otto von Bismarck as his prime minister. Bismarck sought the unification of Germany under Prussia's leadership. To reach this goal, he drew Prussia into wars with Denmark and Austria. His victories in these conflicts

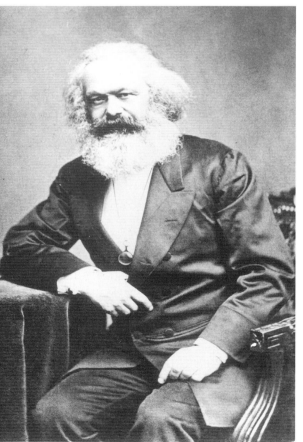

Photo by Bildarchiv Preussischer Kulturbesitz

In 1848 the German writer Karl Marx published *The Communist Manifesto,* which called for ownership of factories by industrial laborers and rule by the proletariat (working class). Believing his ideas to be dangerous, the government of Prussia expelled Marx in the next year.

gave Bismarck the authority he needed to replace the German Confederation with a new state, the North German Confederation, which Prussia dominated.

At the same time, a member of the Hohenzollern dynasty was claiming the throne of Spain. This action caused conflict with France, which feared Hohenzollern domination of Europe as well as Prussia's growing military might. Seeing another opportunity to strengthen his state, Bismarck sparked the Franco-Prussian War in 1870. The war ended with the fall of Paris, the French capital, in 1871. After France surrendered, Bismarck forced the French government to make heavy war reparations (payments). The French also had to surrender the region of Alsace-Lorraine, a territory on the west bank of the Rhine River.

During the Franco-Prussian War, Bismarck brought the southern German states under Prussian control. Wilhelm assumed the leadership of the now unified German Empire as Kaiser (emperor) Wilhelm I. A new constitution established a two-house legislature, but this body had little political power.

In the late nineteenth century, Germany experienced rapid growth. The population

Engineers in a Berlin factory examine plans for a steam locomotive. The building of a nationwide train network laid the foundation for Germany's rapid industrialization in the late nineteenth century.

increased, and busy mines and factories transformed the nation's economy. Germany established colonies in Africa and Asia to match the growing international power of Britain and France.

Bismarck kept firm control over the legislature and tried to stamp out opposition to the Prussian monarchy. He also limited the activities of the Socialist party, which championed the rights of Germany's industrial workers. But the rapid industrialization of the country fostered a strong labor movement and widespread support of Socialist politicians.

War and Defeat

Industrialization in Europe brought about an intense rivalry for land and trade among the European powers. The leaders of Germany realized that this competition could easily end in conflict. Wilhelm II, who became Germany's ruler in 1888, ordered the construction of a powerful, modern navy. Germany, Austria, and Italy had already formed the Triple Alliance and had agreed to cooperate in case of war. Fearing Germany's military power, Russia, France, and Britain later signed the Triple Entente. The two competing blocs built up their forces and prepared for a continent-wide conflict.

In June 1914, the heir to the throne of Austria was murdered in Serbia, a region in southeastern Europe. Austria reacted by declaring war on Serbia, an ally of Russia. In defense of Serbia, the nations of the Triple Entente quickly mobilized their forces. Germany also put its troops on a war footing to honor its alliance with Austria. In August Wilhelm II ordered an attack on France, an action that brought the two European alliances into World War I (1914–1918).

In 1869 Ludwig II, the king of Bavaria, hired a designer of theater sets to build the spectacular Neuschwanstein Castle at the foot of the Bavarian Alps. But the expense of building the castle was so great that Ludwig's government nearly went bankrupt. Convinced by this lavish project that their king had lost his mind, Ludwig's ministers forced him from his throne in 1886 and named his uncle, Prince Luitpold, to rule in his place. Within a week, Ludwig died under mysterious circumstances in a nearby lake.

Although Germany defeated Russia on the eastern front, the United States joined the nations of the Triple Entente in 1917. British, French, and U.S. forces fought Germany to a stalemate in northern France. But with their supplies cut off by a sea blockade, Wilhelm's commanders gradually lost ground. In November 1918, Germany surrendered.

Angered by the defeat, German workers and soldiers staged riots throughout the country. Kaiser Wilhelm gave up his throne, and the Socialists proclaimed the founding of a new, democratic German government. Under the Treaty of Versailles, Germany returned Alsace-Lorraine to France and surrendered much of eastern Prussia to Poland. The victorious Allies demanded huge reparations and occupied cities and industries in southeastern Germany.

The Weimar Republic

In 1919 an assembly met in Weimar, a city in central Germany, to draw up a new constitution. Led by the Socialists, the assembly established a two-house parliament, an elected presidency, and the office of chancellor, whom the president would appoint. The assembly also ratified (accepted) the Treaty of Versailles.

Burdened by the heavy war reparations, the German economy suffered collapse during the 1920s. Unemployment rose, and raging inflation destroyed the value of German currency. As Germans lost faith in the country's leaders, small but violent political parties sprang up to fuel the turmoil. In 1923 the National Socialist (Nazi) party, led by Adolf Hitler, attempted to stage a *putsch* (overthrow) in Munich.

Photo by Bildarchiv Preussischer Kulturbesitz

An unemployed woman seeks work from passersby on a Berlin street. A worldwide depression caused widespread joblessness in Germany during the early 1930s.

A hero of World War I, Paul von Hindenburg became president of the Weimar Republic in 1925. Unable to stem the rising popularity of the Nazi party, Hindenburg named Nazi leader Adolf Hitler chancellor in 1933. This action paved the way for the Nazi takeover of the German government.

Courtesy of German Information Center

33

Although the revolt failed, Hitler and the Nazi party steadily gained support.

Under the leadership of President Paul von Hindenburg, the German economy improved in the late 1920s. But a worldwide depression that began in 1929 dealt another blow to the Weimar Republic. Street fighting among Nazis, Communists, and other groups increased. In the early 1930s, Hindenburg began ruling the country by decree, while the legislature lost power.

The Nazi Regime

After serving a short jail term for his role in the Munich revolt, Hitler began giving angry public speeches, in which he blamed Communists, Jews, and other groups for Germany's wartime defeat and for its economic problems. Many Germans agreed with these views, and the Nazi party's power and popularity increased. Bowing to public pressure, Hindenburg appointed Hitler chancellor in 1933.

Courtesy of U. S. Army

Adolf Hitler, leader of the Nazi party, returns a salute to members of the German parliament. With the party exercising complete control over the legislature, Hitler's orders automatically became law.

After Hindenburg's death in 1934, Hitler named himself Germany's *führer* (leader) and took complete control of German industry, administration, and education. The Nazis set up a state police force known as the Gestapo and built concentration camps for political prisoners. Jews and others whom the Nazis considered enemies of the regime lost their homes, businesses, jobs, and citizenship.

Germany rapidly strengthened its army and navy, denounced the Treaty of Versailles, and began claiming territory in neighboring nations. In 1938 Hitler forced Austria to unite with Nazi Germany. He also allied with Italy and Japan, forming the Axis powers. To avoid another war,

Courtesy of Library of Congress

Adolf Hitler (seventh from left) **and members of the Nazi party march beneath huge banners bearing the party's insignia. Street parades and massive rallies increased Hitler's popularity during the 1930s.**

34

Britain and France then signed an agreement allowing Germany to take over part of Czechoslovakia, a nation that had been created after the breakup of Austria-Hungary in 1918.

In 1939 Germany signed a pact with the Soviet Union, a vast Communist nation to the east. Although they agreed not to attack one another, these two countries secretly planned to invade and divide Poland. Fearing an attack, Poland mobilized its armies. When Hitler launched World War II by invading Poland on September 1, Britain and France declared war on Germany. Poland's poorly equipped forces were quickly defeated, and Germany and the Soviet Union occupied the country.

World War II and Its Aftermath

After defeating Poland, Hitler ordered invasions of Denmark, Norway, Belgium, the Netherlands, and France. He also broke the 1939 treaty by attacking the Soviet Union. German and Italian armies overran southeastern Europe and much of North Africa. In December 1941, Japan attacked the United States, a military and industrial power that immediately joined the Allies of France, Britain, and the Soviet Union in their war against the Axis.

By the winter of 1942, Germany had conquered most of Europe, including the western plains of the Soviet Union. In many occupied areas, the Germans seized industries, crop harvests, and natural

Artwork by Laura Westlund

German and Italian armies had conquered most of Europe by the summer of 1942. But after Hitler declared war on the Soviet Union, Germany had to fight on western and eastern fronts. In the spring of 1945, the combined forces of the Allies overwhelmed Germany's military.

Courtesy of Library of Congress

Women crowd the barracks of Belsen, a concentration camp in northwestern Germany for political and military prisoners. Allied troops liberated Belsen on April 14, 1945, just three weeks before the end of World War II.

resources and made conquered peoples work as slave laborers. As the war progressed, German forces herded Jews, Slavs, Gypsies, and political and military prisoners into concentration camps, where millions of inmates were put to death.

But German armies were fighting on several fronts, and the United States was scoring victories against Japan in the Pacific Ocean. While Allied bombers attacked German factories, railroads, and cities, counterattacks forced Germany out of the Soviet Union and North Africa. In June 1944, Allied armies invaded France and drove the Germans from Paris. With Soviet armies marching on Berlin and the war nearly lost, Hitler committed suicide on April 30, 1945. One week later, Germany formally surrendered.

Britain, France, the United States, and the Soviet Union divided the nation and the capital city of Berlin into occupation zones. With its industries destroyed and many of its cities in ruins, Germany had to depend on aid from its former enemies to survive and rebuild.

Postwar Divisions

In 1948 the United States, France, and Britain merged their three occupation zones while maintaining control over West Berlin. The Soviet Union still occupied eastern Germany and East Berlin. With Soviet forces backing them, German Communist and Socialist leaders formed the Socialist Unity party and set up a government to administer the eastern zone.

The Allies allowed German politicians to establish a new, democratic government in Bonn. This city on the Rhine River became the capital of the Federal Republic of Germany (West Germany) in 1949. The eastern sector of Berlin became the capital of the Soviet-controlled zone, where the German Communists founded the German Democratic Republic (East Germany). Berlin remained divided into western and eastern halves.

To help the war-ravaged nations of Europe and the new West German state, the United States adopted the Marshall Plan, a program of financial aid and investment. The West German government drew up a new constitution, and a parliament began meeting in Bonn. The legislature elected Konrad Adenauer, the leader of the Christian Democratic Union (CDU), as the Federal Republic's first chancellor.

Adenauer forged close economic and political ties with the nations of western Europe. In 1955 West Germany joined the United States and several western European nations in the North Atlantic Treaty Organization (NATO), a military alliance.

In East Germany, the government took control of banks, industries, farms, and private businesses. Walter Ulbricht, the general secretary (leader) of the Socialist Unity party, remained East Germany's most powerful politician throughout the 1950s and 1960s. Under Ulbricht's guidance, East Germany became a founding member of the Warsaw Pact. This alliance of Europe's Communist nations also included the Soviet Union, Hungary, Poland, Czechoslovakia, Bulgaria, and Romania.

The Cold War

In 1955 the Allied occupation of Germany ended. Germany and Berlin became the dividing line in Europe between democratic countries allied with NATO and Communist nations dominated by the Soviet Union. To prepare for any future conflict, the United States and the Soviet Union based large military forces and

Representatives of the victorious Allies met at the Potsdam Conference in the summer of 1945. The conference turned over the administration of occupied Germany to the United States, Britain, France, and the Soviet Union.

Photo by Drs. A. A. M. van der Heyden, Naarden, the Netherlands

A construction crane rises near the ruins of Dresden's Frauenkirche, which was destroyed during an air raid in 1945. After the war, the city maintained the ruins as a memorial. In the early 1990s, however, the leaders of Dresden decided to rebuild and restore the church.

modern weaponry within Germany. This Cold War (nonviolent conflict) pitted the two blocs against one another and ended most trade and cooperation between them.

East Germany's economic recovery was much weaker than that of West Germany. With the Communist government setting wages and prices, farmers and industrial workers had little incentive to increase their production. Throughout the 1950s, as living standards remained low, millions of East Germans fled to the western sector of Berlin. In 1961, to prevent a further loss of its labor force, the Communist government closed its border with West Germany and built a heavily guarded concrete wall around West Berlin.

With the help of the Marshall Plan, the Federal Republic eventually became one of the richest and most productive nations in the world. Rebuilt factories produced industrial and consumer goods that found a global market. As living standards rose, millions of refugees and *gastarbeiter* (guest workers) from southern Europe and Turkey arrived to meet the increased demand for factory labor.

Photo © Ed King

Police stand atop the Berlin Wall during a street demonstration.

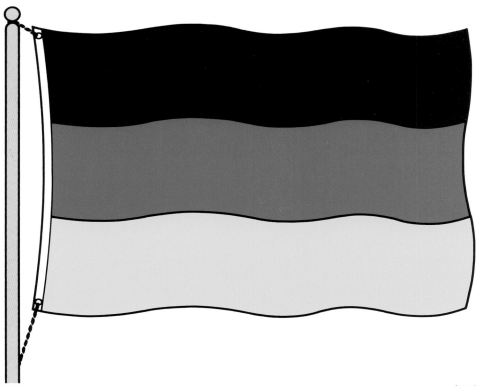

In 1990 reunified Germany officially adopted West Germany's flag. Black, red, and gold have long been associated with German nationalism. According to a popular slogan, these three colors mean "out of the darkness, through blood, and into the sunshine."

Willy Brandt, a member of the Social Democratic party, became West Germany's chancellor in 1969. Brandt's *ostpolitik* (eastern policy) boosted trade and encouraged better relations with the nations of eastern Europe. West Germany established diplomatic links with East Germany in 1973. In the same year, the two countries were admitted separately to the United Nations (UN).

Under Helmut Schmidt, Brandt's successor, West Germany suffered rising inflation and unemployment. In addition, many West Germans began to question their country's participation in NATO. Massive protests against the Cold War took place in West German cities. At the same time, German terrorist groups staged kidnappings of industrialists and government officials.

In East Germany, Erich Honecker succeeded Ulbricht as the Communist party leader in 1971. Honecker stayed closely allied to the Soviet Union but also improved East Germany's links with non-Communist nations. Although its recovery was slower than that of West Germany, East Germany became one of the most productive members of the Warsaw Pact.

Recent Events

In 1982 a vote of "no confidence" by the West German legislature ended Schmidt's term. His successor, Helmut Kohl, maintained West Germany's ties to the east. In 1987 Erich Honecker paid a visit to his birthplace in West Germany. The visit symbolized the hope of many Germans for the reunification of their nation.

Meanwhile, many Communist nations of eastern Europe were suffering economic decline and social unrest. Shortages of food, housing, and consumer goods angered industrial workers, while students and writers demanded more open governments. As the Soviet Union experienced its own political turmoil, its hold over the Warsaw Pact nations weakened.

These events undermined the power of eastern Europe's Communist leaders, including Erich Honecker. The growing unrest in East Germany forced Honecker to resign in October 1989. When Hungary allowed emigrants to cross freely into non-Communist Austria, thousands of East Germans began using this route to flee to West Germany. Unable to stop the migration, the East German government finally opened its borders in November. As the Berlin Wall fell, millions of East Germans crossed into West Berlin.

In March 1990, the East German Communists held open elections, which brought non-Communist political parties to power. Most East Germans favored adopting the economic and political system of West Germany, while most West Germans supported the reunification of the country. After a series of negotiations between leaders of the two states, Germany was formally reunified on October 3, 1990.

Reunification brought a nationwide celebration, as well as immediate economic problems. After losing government support, many inefficient East German businesses failed. At the same time, a worldwide economic slowdown caused German companies to lose foreign markets for their goods. Unemployment rose, and a housing shortage worsened. A flood of refugees in need of jobs and shelter arrived from southeastern Europe, where the fall of Communism had sparked unrest and civil war.

Rising unemployment has caused tension between immigrants and some ethnic Germans. Gangs of violent skinheads, who follow the beliefs and practices of Hitler's Nazi party, have attacked refugees and guest workers. In 1994 the government set harsher penalties for such acts.

Residents of eastern Germany line up near the remains of the Berlin Wall to cross into western Berlin. For 30 years, the heavily guarded wall prevented East Germans from reaching West Berlin and then escaping to western Europe.

Photo © Ed King

Children play among small houses that provide shelter for foreign refugees. The parents of these children claim to suffer political persecution in their homelands. If the German government grants them asylum (legal protection), the family will have the right to settle permanently in Germany.

Also in 1994, Helmut Kohl won another term as federal chancellor. Intent on participating in the European Monetary Unit (EMU), a single European currency for eligible nations, Kohl began attempting to rework Germany's financial situation. Within two years, the government announced austerity measures designed to reduce Germany's federal debt to the level dictated by EMU requirements, which must be met by 1999. Most of the unpopular measures involved cutting workers' benefits, and so German labor unions, already angered by high unemployment, organized a series of strikes in protest.

By 1997 German politicians realized that most of their constituents were against EMU. Few citizens were willing to make the difficult sacrifices required for EMU eligibility. Political infighting, shifting alliances, and flagging popular support of the traditional German political parties have all detracted from the government's efforts at economic reform. Nevertheless Kohl announced he would run for a fifth term as chancellor in October 1998.

The nation is paying a heavy price for reunification, as the government extends financial aid and social benefits to eastern Germany. Although Germany's economy is still one of the world's largest and strongest, its leaders are struggling with difficult social problems.

Government

The 1949 constitution of the Federal Republic (West Germany) governs the unified nation of Germany. Representatives of the German *länder* (states) and members of the Bundestag, or parliament, meet every five years to elect the German president, the official head of state. A chancellor, who serves as the head of the German government, selects cabinet ministers and sets policy for nationwide concerns such as defense, foreign affairs, and the federal budget.

Citizens 18 years of age and older elect the 662 members of the Bundestag. The political party that holds a majority in the parliament may nominate the chancellor, who must win election by the entire chamber. The parliament debates important legislation and passes federal laws.

Representatives of the 16 German länder sit on the Bundesrat, or federal council. The council allows the states to approve or reject laws that affect local governments. The heads of the state governments rotate as Bundesrat president, each serving a one-year term.

The German länder have their own legislatures and constitutions. Although the states have the power to pass and enforce local laws, they also must observe statutes passed by the federal government. Länder governments administer health care, education, and environmental policies within their borders. Each state also has its own police force.

The Federal Constitutional Court is Germany's highest court. The Bundestag and Bundesrat each appoint eight judges to the court for 12-year terms. The court reviews laws and policies to make sure they conform with the country's constitution. Five federal courts have the power to review decisions by the local courts. Länder courts hear civil and criminal cases, and lower courts decide administrative disputes.

The nineteenth-century Reichstag in Berlin was the home of Germany's Bundestag (legislature) until the end of World War II. After reunification Germany's leaders decided to move the Bundestag, as well as the entire federal government, from Bonn to Berlin in 1999.

A young girl feeds the pigeons in a Frankfurt square. Germans living in urban areas enjoy strolling through the historic centers of their cities, many of which offer pedestrian zones.

3) The People

Reunification has made Germany the second most populous country in Europe, after Russia. Germany's 82 million people also inhabit one of the continent's most crowded nations. Population density has reached 595 persons per square mile.

In much of western and central Germany, cities and towns dominate the landscape. Many large cities lie close together in industrial zones, such as the Ruhr valley along the upper Rhine River. Large metropolitan areas surround Frankfurt, Munich, Hannover, Berlin, and Stuttgart. The plains of the north and the mountainous regions of the southwest have the country's lowest population density.

Ethnic Germans make up about 95 percent of Germany's population. The

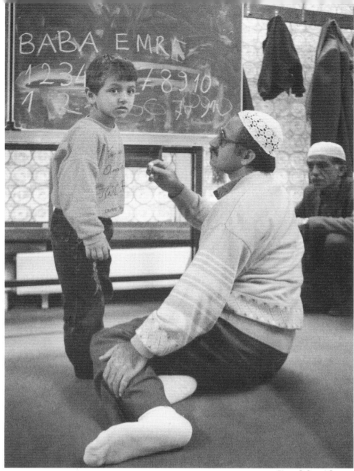

A Turkish immigrant talks to his son during a service at a Berlin mosque (an Islamic house of prayer).

Photo © Stormi Greener

Germans are descendants of ancient northern European peoples—including Slavs, Scandinavians, and Teutons—who migrated across the continent after the fall of the Roman Empire. After World War II, Germany also welcomed people from southern Europe, Turkey, the Middle East, and Africa. Many of these immigrants arrived to fill new factory jobs created by Germany's expanding economy.

In the early 1990s, additional immigrants arrived as Communist regimes fell and as strict border controls ended in eastern Europe. A civil war among Croats, Serbs, and Bosnians in southeastern Europe also brought a wave of refugees to Germany. Immigrants number more than 7 million—almost 9 percent of the country's population. The rising rate of immigration has strained Germany's social-welfare and educational systems. As a result, many politi-

cians are calling for new laws to halt or slow the flow of newcomers.

Health and Education

Germans enjoy good health and an extensive health-care system. Life expectancy is 77 years, an average figure for western Europe. Infant mortality—the number of babies who die before their first birthday—stands at 5.1 deaths for every 1,000 births, also about average for western Europe. A federal system provides health insurance for workers, unemployed people, and retirees. Germans suffering from chronic diseases or who are disabled receive financial assistance.

Heart disease and cancer are the primary causes of death in Germany. Acquired immune deficiency syndrome (AIDS) has also become a growing concern, particularly in urban areas. Although Germany has about 274,000 doctors, rural areas suffer a shortage of physicians. Länder, local communities, and churches run most of Germany's 2,300 hospitals.

Education in Germany begins in the *kindergarten*, a voluntary preschool that accepts students between the ages of three and six. Children then enter a primary school known as a *grundschule*, which lasts for four years.

After the grundschule, students have several options. They can attend a *gymnasium*, a nine-year school that prepares them for university studies, or a *hauptschule*, where they learn academic subjects and trades. Another option is the *realschule*, which offers a slightly more advanced education than the hauptschule. Graduates from a hauptschule or realschule often attend a vocational school that prepares them for careers in industry or business.

Before being admitted to a university, German students must first pass the *abitur*, a difficult examination. About 1.2 million students attend Germany's 83 universities, including the fourteenth-century University of Heidelberg, the country's oldest. All universities are state-run institutions that charge no tuition. Germany also has technical colleges, art institutes, music

Independent Picture Service

Students gather outside a kindergarten in eastern Germany. Like many other schools in the former East Germany, this kindergarten was built as part of a planned city, which also included hospitals, shops, athletic facilities, and parks for the use of residents.

conservatories, theology schools, and continuing-education centers.

Religion

Religion has had a strong influence on Germany's art, politics, music, and literature. For centuries after the crowning of Otto I as the first Holy Roman emperor, Germany

Independent Picture Service

An instructor works with a young violin student in a German music school.

A cow grazes near a carved wooden crucifix in a high Alpine valley. Many such crosses have been built along the roads and hiking trails of southern Germany, a region where the Roman Catholic faith has strong support.

Photo by Ted and Jennifer Olsen

was closely tied to the Roman Catholic Church. Germany was also the birthplace of the Protestant Reformation, in which Martin Luther founded a new branch of Christianity and won a majority of Germans to Protestant churches.

By law people living in Germany may choose and practice any religion. The state provides financial support to the churches, which in turn offer a variety of social services, including preschool education, to their members.

About 45 percent of the German population belong to Protestant sects, including Lutheran and Reformed traditions. Roman Catholics, who form a majority in southern Germany. make up 37 percent of the total population.

Germany's Jewish population numbered about 530,000 before the 1930s. After Hitler rose to power, however, the Nazi government closed synagogues (Jewish houses of prayer) and forced Jews out of their jobs and homes. Many Jews fled the

The spire of a church rises above a German village.

Photo by Ted and Jennifer Olsen

46

country, and most who remained during World War II were arrested and executed. By the end of the war, only 30,000 Jews had survived within Germany. In the mid-1990s, about 54,000 Jews lived in Germany, mostly in Berlin and Frankfurt.

About 1.7 million Muslims practice the Islamic faith in Germany. Most are ethnic Turks and North Africans who arrived in the country as guest workers. Many refugees from Bosnia, in the former Yugoslavia, also follow Islam.

Language and Literature

German is a member of the Germanic family of languages, which also includes Norwegian, Swedish, Dutch, Danish, and English. Modern German is spoken throughout Germany and Austria and in parts of Switzerland and France. Ethnic Germans living in Romania, Hungary, Poland, and the republics of the former Soviet Union also use German dialects.

By translating the Bible from Hebrew and Greek to German, Martin Luther created a standard written and spoken dialect known as *hochdeutsch,* or High German. All of the country's broadcast and print media use a form of High German. *Plattdeutsch,* or Low German, is commonly heard in northern Germany. Other dialects survive in more isolated rural areas, such as Swabia in southwestern Germany. Residents of the Parisian Islands speak a unique blend of Dutch and German. Yiddish, which originated in Germany, has survived among Jews living in Europe, North America, and the Middle East. In eastern Germany, some ethnic Slavs use German and Slavic words.

Scholars claim that the ninth-century *Hildebrandslied,* the story of a legendary hero, is the oldest literary work in the German language. Other myths and heroic tales of the early Germanic peoples were collected in the *Nibelungenlied.* Around A.D. 1200, many German knights penned epic poems about love and chivalry. *Min-*

nesingers—skilled composers and performers—wrote lyric poetry for performance at royal courts.

German writers flourished after the Protestant Reformation, when poetry, plays, and satirical novels became popular literary forms. Many of these authors used Italian or French works as their models. In the eighteenth century, Gotthold Ephraim Lessing and other writers described the events of their time in their works. Lessing's poetic drama *Nathan der Weise* included a strong appeal for religious tolerance. Younger writers, including Johann Wolfgang von Goethe and Friedrich von Schiller, helped to create a national German literature.

Romantic writers of the 1800s based many of their works on fantasies and folklore. The brothers Jakob and Wilhelm Grimm brought out an edition of traditional children's fairy tales. Many German painters and musicians created works

Jakob *(left)* **and Wilhelm Grimm collected hundreds of German myths and fairy tales for their book** *Grimm's Fairy Tales.* **The brothers also wrote authoritative books on the German language.**

based on E.T.A. Hoffmann's stories of the supernatural. The writer Novalis—whose real name was Friedrich von Hardenberg—authored essays and poetry filled with mystery and religious feeling.

Many German poets and philosophers of the nineteenth century took an interest in Europe's turbulent politics. Heinrich Heine wrote in support of the struggle against Europe's monarchies. Karl Marx and Friedrich Engels set forth the principles of Communism in *Das Kapital* and *The Communist Manifesto*. Friedrich Nietzsche combined poetry and philosophy in his works, which criticized religious faith as well as modern German society.

Europe in the uncertain years before World War I provided the setting for Thomas Mann's *The Magic Mountain*. Hermann Hesse, who fled Germany in 1914 to become a Swiss citizen, incorporated Buddhism and other Asian ideas into *Steppenwolf* and other novels.

Determined to stamp out opposition to their regime, the Nazis banned the books of many prominent German writers. After World War II, Heinrich Böll and Günter Grass faced the legacy of Nazism in their stories and novels. The playwright Bertolt Brecht, who founded his own theater in Berlin, produced satirical plays with political subjects. The works of Christa Wolf, including *Was Bleibt*, describe contemporary life in eastern Germany.

Architecture, Art, and Music

Early German artists and architects borrowed freely from styles popular in other parts of Europe. Thirteenth-century archi-

Independent Picture Service

Bertolt Brecht and the actress Helene Weigel rehearse his play *Mother Courage and Her Children* at the German Theater of Berlin. Brecht fled the Nazi regime in 1933 but after the war returned to East Germany, where he established an acting company known as the Berliner Ensemble.

Frederick the Great hired the finest architects of his day to design and decorate his elaborate summer palace of Sans Souci in Potsdam. These workers are carefully restoring the gilded statues of a Chinese Teahouse, which was built in 1757 in the castle gardens.

Independent Picture Service

tects adopted the Gothic style of northern France to design cathedrals in Cologne and other German cities. Gothic builders used narrow stone buttresses (supports) to strengthen arched ceilings, high stone towers, and windows of stained glass. Painters of the Gothic period combined realistic details of everyday life with subjects from myths and fairy tales.

The Renaissance influenced many of Germany's sixteenth-century artists, including Albrecht Dürer. A master engraver, Dürer also produced portraits and still lifes on canvas. Dürer's works greatly inspired Lucas Cranach, who painted biblical scenes and created portraits of Martin Luther and other Protestant leaders. Matthias Grünewald decorated many German churches and cathedrals with his stained glass, paintings, and altarpieces.

German architects of the eighteenth century favored the elaborate Baroque style popular in France and Italy. Baroque churches and palaces exhibited ornate decor in gold leaf and brightly colored marble. Baroque painters enjoyed using mythological subjects in their large and detailed canvases.

German painters of the 1800s, including Caspar David Friedrich, turned to Romanticism, a style in which dark colors and serious subjects revealed the heroic inner struggles of the individual. In the early

Independent Picture Service

Partridge, a watercolor sketch by Albrecht Dürer, displays the remarkable skills of this German artist, who often turned to nature for inspiration.

49

twentieth century, many German artists abandoned Romanticism for Expressionism. The painters Franz Marc, Otto Dix, and Max Beckmann expressed their emotions on canvas by using bright colors and strange, distorted shapes.

The need for extensive postwar rebuilding gave architects a chance to reshape German cities after World War II. One of the most important influences on modern designers was the Bauhaus, a school founded in 1919 by the architect Walter Gropius. Bauhaus designers used steel, concrete, and glass to create stark, geometric structures.

The church as well as the royal courts provided employment to Germany's first professional musicians. Johann Sebastian Bach, a skilled church organist, developed a system of musical harmony that still dominates European music. Bach wrote hundreds of keyboard pieces as well as stirring religious works.

German composers of the nineteenth century were in the forefront of the Romantic movement. Ludwig van Beethoven's dramatic symphonies expanded the harmonic system first laid down by Bach. Robert Schumann and Felix Mendelssohn were known for their "program music," which was based on nonmusical ideas, characters, or stories.

Opera was the most important musical form to Richard Wagner, who drew on German legends and myths in his work. Wagner captivated audiences with *Tristan and Isolde* and *The Ring of the Nibelungen,* a cycle of four operas based on the *Nibelungenlied.*

Other styles of music also thrive in Germany. Berlin hosts an annual jazz festival, and rock bands like Interzone and Die Ärzte are internationally successful. Nina Hagen and Klaus Nomi have won fame for their punk rock performances.

Food

Germans eat large and hearty meals, and each region of the country boasts a food specialty. Bavarians enjoy *knödel* or filled dumplings. Swabia is famous for *spaetzle,* a noodle dish. Cooks in Westphalia prepare cured and smoked ham with dark brown pumpernickel bread. Eel soup, herrings, oysters, and other seafood dishes are popular in the port of Hamburg. Traditional Christmas dinners throughout Germany include roast goose and *stollen,* a fruit bread. Adults drink beer or sweet white wine from the Rhine or Mosel valleys with their main courses.

Several traditional German dishes originated hundreds of years ago. Cooks created sauerkraut—cabbage soaked in brine—to preserve this common vegetable. They also ground up beef, pork, and veal into *wurst,* or sausages.

A German breakfast is usually light, with rolls and jam accompanied by coffee, tea, or milk. Germans traditionally eat a full meal at noon. This *mittagessen* often

Independent Picture Service

A woman shops for fresh fruits and vegetables at an outdoor market.

Diners enjoy the shade and refreshments at a cafe in Berlin. The cafe window advertises *frühstuck* (breakfast) at 8 A.M.

begins with soup, followed by a meat course served with vegetables as well as noodles or dumplings. In recent times, however, the noon meal has become lighter, and many Germans have made the evening meal the largest of the day.

Sports and Recreation

While Germany was a divided nation, athletic clubs in both East and West Germany offered children, teenagers, and adults an opportunity for recreation and team sports. Millions of Germans still belong to at least one sports club, where they can compete with other sports enthusiasts.

Soccer (called *fussball* in German) is the country's most popular sport. Cities, towns, and villages boast their own soccer teams. West Germany's national squad has won the World Cup soccer championship three times and the European championship twice. Germans also compete in

Tourists crowd the narrow streets and alleys of Rothenburg. With several weeks of vacation available to them every year, many Germans spend their free time visiting historic towns and villages.

51

Steffi Graf winds up to serve during a U.S. Open match. Born in Mannheim, Graf first became the top-rated women's tennis player in 1987.

gymnastics, golf, horse riding, and tennis. Bernhard Langer won the Masters golf championship in 1993. Steffi Graf and Boris Becker are among the world's top-rated tennis players.

After World War II, athletes from the former East Germany excelled in Olympic competition. But in 1992 all German Olympic athletes began competing as part of a unified team. At the 1996 Summer Olympics, German athletes won 65 medals, including 20 gold medals. Among the gold medalists were shot putter Astrid Kumbernuss and discus throwers Lars Riedel and Ilke Wyludda.

Recreational sports in Germany include hiking, bicycling, and camping. Canoeists, rowers, sailors, and swimmers use the country's rivers and lakes. Downhill and cross-country skiing are favorite winter sports in the Alps.

Three young athletes display medals they have won in a swimming contest. Each year German schools and cities stage thousands of competitions for students and amateur athletes.

Cargo ships and freight trains crowd the docks of Rostock, a major ship-building center and fishing port on Germany's Baltic coast. The rebuilding of Rostock and other heavily damaged ports after World War II gave a strong boost to Germany's postwar economy.

4) The Economy

In the 1930s and 1940s, German industry came under the strict control of the Nazi government and turned from civilian to military production. But the bombing of Germany during World War II demolished industrial zones, transportation systems, and residential areas. The German economy came to a standstill, and millions suffered unemployment and poverty.

After the war, the U.S.-sponsored Marshall Plan brought about the rebuilding of West Germany. New industries in the region prospered, and, as a wide variety of consumer goods became available, the standard of living rapidly improved.

In East Germany, the postwar Communist government refused western aid and took direct control of industries and agriculture. Although industrialization helped the region to recover from the war, shortages of food and consumer goods quickly developed. In the 1980s, the growing inefficiency of the system and the weakness of other Communist regimes in eastern Europe led to the downfall of the East German government.

In the early 1990s, the unified German government took over the economy of eastern Germany. West German money was exchanged for East German currency, and generous social benefits were extended to the eastern population. Most state-owned businesses were sold to private investors. Germany's economy boomed as easterners rushed to buy consumer goods, then slumped with a worldwide recession. Construction in the east helped fuel another boom in 1994, but another recession followed. These fluctuations have resulted in a 12.2 percent unemployment rate, and Germany's eligibility for the single European currency is increasingly uncertain.

But the country has the most productive industries, and one of the largest economies, in Europe. Although disparity continues between east and west, eastern Germany is catching up. In the late 1990s, economists projected improvements in Germany's apparently stabilized economy.

Manufacturing

The manufacturing sector drove Germany's recovery after World War II. West German companies expanded rapidly to meet the growing need for consumer goods, heavy machinery, cars, textiles, and electrical equipment. Automaking boosted Germany's foreign trade, while the chemical, steel, and food-processing industries also produced exports. By the mid-1990s, the manufacturing sector provided 25 percent of the country's jobs.

The densely populated Ruhr valley, in northwestern Germany, has long been the country's principal industrial region. Extensive reserves of coal in the area supply the Ruhr's huge steel plants, which turn out the raw material for construction and

Two autoworkers assemble a vehicle in a German plant. Germany's high-quality cars make up a large percentage of the country's exports.

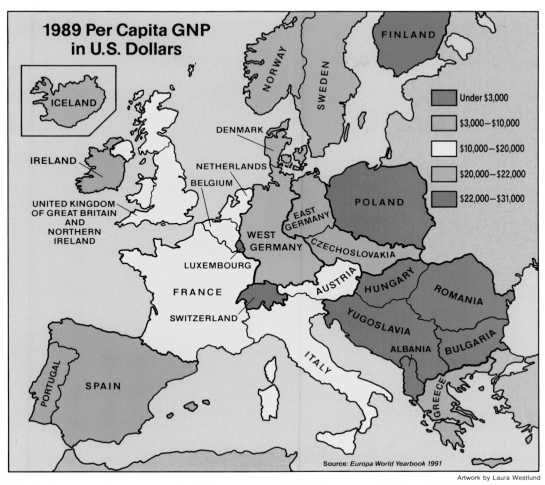

1989 Per Capita GNP in U.S. Dollars

Under $3,000
$3,000–$10,000
$10,000–$20,000
$20,000–$22,000
$22,000–$31,000

Source: *Europa World Yearbook 1991*

Artwork by Laura Westlund

This chart compares the average productivity per person—calculated by gross national product (GNP) per capita—for 26 European countries. The GNP is the value of all goods and services produced by a country in a year. In 1989 West Germany enjoyed a much higher rate of productivity than East Germany. But reunification has led to increased manufacturing in the east, where new investment has greatly changed the region's economy. The per-capita GNP of the combined Germanies reached $27,510 in 1995.

for automobiles, ships, and machinery. Ruhr factories also produce chemicals, machinery, rubber, and textiles.

Workers in Berlin process food and beverages and make electrical goods and textiles. The shipyards of Bremerhaven, Kiel, and Hamburg construct oil tankers, fishing boats, cargo ships, and ferries. German industries also make clothing, furniture, scientific instruments, cameras, computers, toys, and leather goods. German aero-

space companies cooperate with several other European nations to produce the Airbus, a popular passenger plane.

Although many eastern German companies have gone bankrupt, the region offers important advantages to firms from western Germany and from the rest of western Europe. Because the former Communist government tightly controlled prices and wages, production costs in the eastern zone have remained low. Several western

With the help of computerized monitoring systems, German farmers control the spraying of chemical pesticides on their fields.

German automakers are opening plants in eastern Germany, which has also attracted joint ventures with other European nations.

Agriculture, Fishing, and Forestry

Since World War II, the number of farms in Germany has steadily decreased, although half of the country's land remains under cultivation. Mechanization has increased productivity, and by the early 1990s each German farmer was producing enough crops to feed 75 people. Nevertheless, Germany still must import about one-third of its food supply.

German farms are small, averaging about 22 acres in size. Many farmers work their land only part time and supplement their income with jobs in nearby cities and factories. Some larger farms have joined cooperatives, in which workers pool their resources and share the profits from the sale of livestock and crops.

Crop and livestock production varies by region. Fruit orchards thrive in the Rhine

A young farmer holds two lambs at a sheep-raising operation. Each of the ranch's animals provides about 14 pounds of wool every year.

Courtesy of German Information Center

German botanists test hydroponic gardening, in which plants feed on water and dissolved nutrients. This method allows food crops to be grown without soil.

River Valley, while potatoes, grains, and fruit grow in the Thuringian Basin. Grape vineyards stretch along the banks of the Rhine, Mosel, and Neckar rivers. Many farmers along the northern seacoast raise horses or dairy cattle. Beef cattle and sheep graze in the pastures of the Alpine foothills.

After World War II, East Germany organized its private farms into about 5,000 large, state-run cooperatives. In the early 1990s, the government of Germany ended these policies by selling acreages to individual farmers and turning the cooperatives into private companies. Nevertheless, many eastern German farmers cannot compete with the efficient, mechanized farms of western Germany. To help integrate German agriculture, the government

provides financial support to newly privatized farms in the eastern zone.

Germany's fishing industry is centered around its North Sea ports, including Bremerhaven, one of the busiest fishing centers in Europe. The most important catches are herring, cod, sole, and flounder. German boats work in the North Sea, the Baltic Sea, and the North Atlantic Ocean near the coast of Greenland. Overfishing by Germany and by other European fleets, however, has depleted fish stocks in many of these areas.

Forests cover nearly one-third of Germany's land and provide about two-thirds of the country's lumber and paper products. Workers on government-controlled plantations carefully plan and monitor timber growth. Since 1975 the government

Engineers at a coal-fired power plant examine a control panel. Germany has developed hydropower, nuclear power, and other forms of electricity, and coal plants provide a much smaller percentage of the nation's energy than in the past.

has also required forestry companies to replant harvested areas. Despite these efforts at preservation, severe air pollution from German factories has damaged the country's forests. In addition heavy storms in 1990 uprooted or damaged nearly half of western Germany's woodlands.

Mining and Energy

Coal deposits near the Ruhr River became the mainstay of German industry during the 1800s. The Ruhr coalfields supplied fuel for merchant ships, steam locomotives, and steel factories. By the 1970s, mining companies had dug up much of the country's high-quality coal. Remaining reserves have proved expensive to extract. Germany still has large supplies of rock salt and of potash, an important ingredient in the making of agricultural fertilizers. Other mineral deposits include lead, copper, tin, uranium, and zinc.

Eastern Germany's largest mineral resource is lignite coal. Found mainly in Sax-

ony and in southern Brandenburg, lignite is used to generate electricity and as a raw material in the chemical industry. The heavy smoke created by lignite burning led to serious environmental damage in East Germany, which lacked pollution-control equipment.

Coal contributes less than one-fifth of Germany's total energy production. There are also small deposits of oil in the northern plains and in the foothills of the Alps, and energy companies have found natural gas beneath the floor of the North Sea. Nevertheless, Germany must import nearly all of its crude oil and most of its natural gas.

The German government is supporting the development of new energy sources, such as solar power and wind energy. In western Germany, 21 nuclear power stations provided 33 percent of the country's electricity during the mid to late 1990s. Many of the older reactors in the eastern zone, however, are considered unsafe and have been shut down.

Transportation and Tourism

The reunification of Germany and the elimination of closed borders in eastern Europe have made the nation a key link in the European transportation network. Germany's rail system uses about 25,200 miles of track, of which 11,300 miles are electrified. An urban train called the S-Bahn provides commuter service in the nation's largest cities. Many cities also have subway systems and bus networks.

The country's modern highways date to the 1930s, when the Nazi regime built a fast, four-lane roadway known as the *autobahn*. Autobahns, which make up a 6,900-mile network, have no official speed limit.

Germany's merchant fleet includes more than 800 ships. Cargo ships and passenger ferries call at Hamburg, Bremen, Wilhelmshaven, and several other seaports. A canal links the Rhine, Main, and Danube rivers, providing a route for river freight across Europe from the North Sea to the Black Sea.

Germany's largest airport, at Frankfurt, has become an important hub for European air traffic. Airports at Frankfurt and several other major cities handle both domestic and international flights. The national airline, Lufthansa, flies a modern fleet of passenger planes to destinations around the world.

The country's roads, ships, and planes bring in millions of traveling foreigners, who contribute about $8 billion every year to Germany's economy. The capitals of Germany's former principalities attract visitors who explore palaces, cathedrals, civic buildings, and castles. Even small villages boast historic churches and central market squares, where officials have taken care to preserve original street plans and architecture.

Photo by Erwin C. "Bud" Nielsen

Tugboats dock at Hamburg harbor, one of the largest ports in Europe. The small but powerful boats maneuver freighters, tankers, and other vessels through the busy channels of the harbor, which lies 68 miles from the North Sea on the Elbe River.

Photo by Bernice K. Condit

Linderhof, the smallest of the many castles built by King Ludwig II, sits between a mountain and an elegant reflecting pool. The gilded statue of the sea god Neptune in the pool encloses a fountain that shoots a jet of water more than 100 feet into the air.

Tourists also seek natural attractions, such as the North Sea coast, the Harz Mountains of central Germany, the Black Forest, and Lake Constance. Cruising boats follow the course of the Rhine River, where ruined castles loom over the valley's cliffs and hillsides. More than 80 special routes guide visitors away from major traffic arteries. The Romantic Road, for example, winds past Dinkelsbühl and other historic towns.

Many German cities host annual festivals. Every 10 years, visitors to the Bavarian village of Oberammergau can see a play that commemorates the village's survival of a deadly plague in 1632. During the 16 days of Oktoberfest in Munich, beer tents offer local brews as well as lively sideshows, musical performances, and bazaars. Since 1876 the Bavarian town of

Bayreuth, where Richard Wagner lived and worked, has attracted thousands of people with performances of Wagnerian operas.

Foreign Trade

The postwar division of Germany created two separate economies with different trading links. East Germany exported its goods to other members of the Soviet bloc in central and eastern Europe. In 1957 West Germany joined the European Union (EU), a group of non-Communist nations that pursued common trade and economic policies. This action strengthened West Germany's economy by increasing its exports to other EU nations.

West Germany's rapid postwar growth eventually made it the largest exporter in Europe. The country's high standard

Workers maintain equipment at a machine-tool factory in eastern Germany. The lower wages and operating costs in what was once East Germany are attracting many foreign companies and investors to the area.

of living and its strong demand for consumer goods have also created an important market for foreign importers. A reunified Germany sells more goods than it buys, giving the nation a trade surplus.

Germany exports vehicles, chemicals, optical instruments, electrical equipment, heavy machinery, and food. Major imports include energy products, clothing, textiles, food, and machinery. The country's most

Cargo stands ready for loading through the nose hatch of a German plane. These aircraft, which can carry up to 100 tons of freight, form an important link in Germany's international trade.

A delivery driver rolls a barrel of beer toward a restaurant. Germany produces internationally renowned beers and is one of the biggest beer-consuming nations in the world.

important trading partners include France, Italy, the Netherlands, the United States, Belgium and Luxembourg, the United Kingdom, Japan, Austria, and Switzerland.

By the mid to late 1990s, after a slump earlier in the decade, exports were growing strongly and productivity was increasing. Forecasts for continued foreign trade looked favorable.

An ancient castle looms near the Lorelei Rock on the banks of the Rhine River. According to a popular German tale, the water nymph Lorelei lured passing sailors to their deaths with her bewitching singing.

Photo by Erwin C. "Bud" Nielsen

Cafes and traditional homes line the streets of a town in the Mosel River Valley.

The Future

Germany's recovery and reunification have brought the country economic and political leadership in Europe. As the most prosperous nation of the EU, Germany can greatly influence this organization, which plans to end Europe's trade barriers and to issue a single European currency.

But Germany's prosperity and continued economic recovery depend on strong exports. If foreign markets slow down, the country's growth could be seriously hurt. Nevertheless Germany has made steady gains, and the nation's economic problems are expected to lessen in the next few years.

At the same time, popular dissatisfaction with the country's leadership has cast uncertainty on German politics. The nation is still feeling the social, political, and economic aftershocks of reunification, and these effects may continue for a decade or more. Germans must keep their goals firmly in sight to assure a prosperous future.

Photo by Erwin C. "Bud" Nielsen

Glass-walled skyscrapers are common in Frankfurt, a thriving center of German banking and industry.

Index